I0636713

EDENDERRY

. 3 NOV 2022

WITHDRAWN

J613.2

16/9862

16 - 393

613.94

Wants versus Needs

Food and Drink

Linda Staniford

raintree

a Capstone company — publishers for children

Raintree is an imprint of Capstone Global Library Limited, a company incorporated in England and Wales having its registered office at 7 Pilgrim Street, London, EC4V 6LB – Registered company number: 6695582

www.raintreepublishers.co.uk
myorders@raintreepublishers.co.uk

Text © Capstone Global Library Limited 2015
The moral rights of the proprietor have been asserted.

All rights reserved. No part of this publication may be reproduced in any form or by any means (including photocopying or storing it in any medium by electronic means and whether or not transiently or incidentally to some other use of this publication) without the written permission of the copyright owner, except in accordance with the provisions of the Copyright, Designs, and Patents Act 1988 or under the terms of a licence issued by the Copyright Licensing Agency, Saffron House, 6–10 Kirby Street, London EC1N 8TS (www.cla. co.uk). Applications for the copyright owner's written permission should be addressed to the publisher.

Edited by Linda Staniford and Shelly Lyons
Designed by Philippa Jenkins
Original illustrations © Capstone Global Library Ltd 2014
Picture research by Tracy Cummins
Production by Helen McCreath
Originated by Capstone Global Library Ltd
Printed and bound in China

ISBN 978 1 406 29059 2
18 17 16 15 14
10 9 8 7 6 5 4 3 2 1

British Library Cataloguing in Publication Data
A full catalogue record for this book is available from the British Library.

Acknowledgements
We would like to thank the following for permission to reproduce photographs: Capstone Press: Karon Dubke, 8, 17, 22 Bottom, 23C, Philippa Jenkins, Cover Left, Design Elements; Getty Images: Image Source, 18; Shutterstock: Christian Draghici, 7, Fanfo, 9, Gladskikh Tatiana, 19, Hurst Photo, 10, 23D, Jacek Chabraszewski, 6, Kzenon, 12, 23B, lightwavemedia, 20, M. Unal Ozmen, 16, Maks Narodenko, 1, Cover Right, Marc Dietrich, 14, Monkey Business Images, 13, 15, 21, 23E, Back Cover, Nitr, 22 Top, Ruth Black, 11, Tatyana Vyc, 4, 23A, Thomas M Perkins, 5.

Every effort has been made to contact copyright holders of material reproduced in this book. Any omissions will be rectified in subsequent printings if notice is given to the publisher.

Disclaimer
All the internet addresses (URLs) given in this book were valid at the time of going to press. However, due to the dynamic nature of the internet, some addresses may have changed, or sites may have changed or ceased to exist since publication. While the author and publisher regret any inconvenience this may cause readers, no responsibility for any such changes can be accepted by either the author or the publisher.

Contents

Some words are shown in bold, **like this**. You can find them in the glossary on page 23.

What are needs and wants?

Needs are things we cannot live without. We need food and drink for **energy** and to keep our bodies working properly.

Wants are things we would like to have.
Some kinds of food and drink are wants.
Chocolate is a food you may want but
do not need.

What foods do we need to eat?

We need to eat **healthy** foods that will make us grow strong and give us **energy**. This will help to keep our bodies working well.

Too much of the wrong food is not good for you. You may want a burger and chips, but that is not a healthy meal!

What foods will make us grow?

Our bodies need **protein** to grow. Protein is in foods like meat, fish, nuts, eggs and beans. You need to eat some protein each day.

We may want to eat fried meat or fish.
But fried food is not **healthy**.

What foods will give us energy?

We need to eat starchy foods that give us **energy**. Bread, rice and pasta all have **starch**. You need to eat some of these things each day.

Cakes and biscuits give us lots of
energy. But this energy comes from
sugar and fat. Too much sugar and fat
is bad for us.

What foods will keep us healthy?

We need to eat foods that keep us looking and feeling **healthy**. Fruit and vegetables help to do this. You need to eat different kinds of fruit and vegetables each day.

Fruit and vegetables have
vitamins. Our bodies need
vitamins to stay healthy.

What can we eat between meals?

You may want to eat snacks, such as crisps. These taste nice, but you should not eat them too often. They have a lot of fat, which is bad for your heart.

If you feel hungry between meals, you should choose a **healthier** snack. You could eat some vegetable sticks or nuts.

Is sugar bad for us?

Ice cream, sweets and chocolate taste good, but they are sugary. Sugar is bad for your teeth and your body.

Instead of sweets, you could eat some fruit. Fruit has some sugar, but it also has **vitamins**, which your body needs.

What can we drink?

You might want to drink fizzy drinks that taste sweet and bubbly. But these drinks often have a lot of sugar in them. Fruit juice has a lot of sugar, too.

If you are thirsty, the best drink is water. You need to drink plenty of water each day. Water satisfies your thirst and keeps you **healthy**.

Can we have some of the foods that are bad for us?

You can eat some crisps, cake and ice cream. But you should not eat these foods too often.

You need to make sure that you eat **healthy** foods every day.

Quiz

Which of these meals do you want, and which do you need?

Picture glossary

energy the power to be active

healthy being fit and well

protein food that makes your body grow

starch one type of food that gives you energy

vitamins substances found in food such as fruit and vegetables, that help keep your body healthy

Index

Note to parents and teachers

Reading non-fiction texts for information is an important part of a child's literary development. Readers can be encouraged to ask simple questions and then use the text to find the answers. Each chapter in this book begins with a question. Read the questions together. Look at the pictures. Talk about what the answer might be. Then read the text to find out if your predictions were correct. To develop readers' enquiry skills, encourage them to think of other questions they might ask about the topic. Discuss where you could find the answers. Assist children in using the contents page, picture glossary and index to practise research skills and new vocabulary.

4

EDENDERRY

. 3 NOV 2022

WITHDRAWN